Kids in Their Communities

I Live in a Town

Stasia Ward Kehoe

The Rosen Publishing Group's
PowerKids Press™
New York

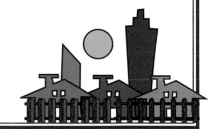

For Kevin, Thomas, and Mak

Published in 2000 by The Rosen Publishing Group, Inc.
29 East 21st Street, New York, NY 10010

First Edition

Book Design: Michael de Guzman

Photo Credits and Photo Illustrations: pp. 4, 7, 8, 11, 12, 16, 20 by Binney K. Wells; p. 15 CORBIS/ James P. Blair; p. 19 CORBIS/Jim McDonald.

Kehoe, Stasia Ward, 1968–
     I live in a town / Stasia Ward Kehoe.
     p. cm — (Kids in their communities)
   Summary: An eight-year-old child who lives in a small town in New Hampshire describes life in that rural community including its homes, schools, town meetings, orchards, and special days.
     ISBN 0-8239-5440-4
     1. New Hampshire—Social life and customs Juvenile literature. 2. City and town life—New Hampshire Juvenile literature. 3. Children—New Hampshire—Social life and customs Juvenile literature. 4. City and town life—New England—Juvenile literature. [1. New Hampshire—Social life and customs. 2. City and town life—New Hampshire.] I. Title. II. Series: Kehoe, Stasia Ward, 1968– Kids in their communities.
F34.3.K44 1999
974.2—dc21   99-25627
                                                       CIP

Manufactured in the United States of America

CONTENTS

Doak

My name is Doak. I am eight years old. My family and I live in a town. A town is smaller than a city, but it is still run by its own **government**. My town is in the state of New Hampshire. New Hampshire is in the part of the United States that is called New England. I learned at school that many of America's first settlers came to New England because there was lots of land for farming. Many of the towns and cities in New England grew out of these early settlements.

In a small town like mine, there are lots of trees to climb and places to play.

New England Towns

Early New England towns were each built around a square. At first, the square was a grassy area where cows, sheep, and horses could graze. In the 1800s, towns changed. Town halls, churches, and shops were put up around the square. The town square became the center of **community** life because that is where people went to shop, visit, pray, or discuss what was happening in the town.

This covered bridge crosses one of the rivers in my town. ▶

My House

My house is more than 100 years old. Some houses on my street are older than that, and some are newer. One thing all the houses have in common is that they are built far enough away from the road to have a big front yard. New England was the first place where houses were built in this way. Later, lots of towns across the United States followed this example. People built houses with big yards just like the ones we have in New England.

◄ *My family loves its old house, and the front yard is a great place to play.*

Getting Around

The center of my town has a fire department, a bank, a gas station, a grocery store, a video store, and a pizza **parlor**. To find a mall or movie theater, we need to drive to a larger town or city. Many moms and dads from my town work in nearby cities, like Concord, which is the **capital** of New Hampshire. There are no trains, and almost no buses or taxis. People drive cars to get where they want to go.

We visit the center of town to run errands.

School

I am in the third grade at school. One of the neat things about going to school in my town is our special ski program. On Wednesdays, students get out of school early to take ski lessons. Skiing is a popular sport in New England. Cross-country skiing is done across flat land. Downhill skiing is when you ski down the slopes of steep mountains. When I am older and go to high school, I want to be on the ski team.

At my school, there are about 70 students in each grade. The school has kindergarten through third grade.

The Orchard

My grandparents own an **orchard**. Sometimes I help watch my younger sisters while my mom works in the orchard store. She sells apples and peaches grown in the orchard. You can get other things at the store, too, like **cider**, apple pie, and small gifts. People from my town like to visit the store and pick fruit from the orchard. Classes from my school visit the orchard to learn about how fruits grow.

People like to pick apples from the trees in the orchard. ▶

Town Meeting

Once a year, my parents go to a town meeting. The town meeting is a chance for people to talk about the way they think the town should be run. At the meeting, people talk about how to raise money for schools and road **repairs**. They vote on laws. They also talk about what the people in the town government are doing. Anybody who owns land in our town has the right to go to the town meeting and **vote** on town issues.

◀ *There are offices for town officials in the town hall, but the town meeting is held at the high school.*

Special Days

Every summer, our town **hosts** the Hopkinton State Fair. It's lots of fun. The fair lasts one week. People from all over the state bring their horses, cows, pigs, sheep, and even **llamas**. The animals are put into contests and the owners of the finest animals win prizes. People also **display** their best fruits, vegetables, jams, and jellies. There are **carnival** rides, barbecues, tractor pulls, musicians, and crafts. My brother Zakry and I love to eat the homemade fudge!

The Hopkinton State Fair has lots of fun rides. ▶

A Special Place

One of my favorite places in town is our new library. Many people in my town **donated** money, time, and ideas to help make the finished library a wonderful place. The library has great books and computers. It also has a fireplace and a community room for story hours and interesting talks. I like to sit on one of the couches and read a good book!

The new library has great books that I can read for school reports or just for fun.

Life in a Town

Today, we have cars, computers, and cable television instead of horses, feather pens, and dinners cooked by the fire, but in many ways my town is a lot like it was two hundred years ago. People still build big houses with big front yards. People still buy apples at the orchard. People still give their opinions at the town meeting. Best of all, when I walk down the street, everybody knows me and stops to say hello.

Glossary

capital (KA-pih-tul) Where the government of a place is located.

carnival (KAR-nih-vul) A group of games, rides, and activities moved from place to place.

cider (SY-dur) A drink made by pressing apples.

community (kuh-MYOO-nih-tee) A group of people who share things in common and help to care for one another.

display (dih-SPLAY) To set up for others to see.

donated (DOH-nay-tid) When something is given to help others.

government (GUH-vurn-mint) The people who make laws for how a place will be run.

hosts (HOSTS) To provide a place for an activity.

llamas (LAH-muhz) South American animals that are related to the camel but do not have humps.

orchard (OR-churd) An area where fruit trees are grown.

parlor (PAR-lur) A place where a business, such as a restaurant, is run.

repairs (ruh-PEHRZ) Adjustments to fix something that is broken.

vote (VOHT) To give a formal opinion on a matter.

Index

Web Site:

http://www.visitnh.gov/